GU00597467

Troon

in old picture postcards

by
Stewart C. Wyllie
and
James Wilson

European Library – Zaltbommel/Netherlands

GB ISBN 90 288 4890 8 / CIP

© 1990 European Library – Zaltbommel/Netherlands

INTRODUCTION

Troon is a small traditional modern town with very little history, the main town centre only dating from the early 1800's. Before then it was a small coastal hamlet between Irvine and Ayr in the parish of Dundonald and consisting of a few small farms, fishermens cottages and an inn.

The name Troon was probably taken from the Gaelic 'AN – Trone', meaning 'The Nose' or 'The Bill'. The spelling of Troon had changed over the years: Trune, Trone, Tryne and Trwyn.

Smuggling was rife on Troon's shoreline. Matthew Hay and his cronies used the north shore near where the salt pans were, to land his contraband spirits, tobacco etc.; from there it was spirited away to Loans, Dundonald, Collenan and beyond, some times just ahead of the excise men and soldiers.

Troon, in the early days, was owned by the Fullarton family, in 1344 they were granted a charter from King Robert II, granting them the lands of Crosbie, Lady Isle and Orangefield which they owned till 1805 when it was sold to the Marquis of Titchfield, afterwards known as the 4th Duke of Portland, Marquis of Ailsa.

In 1707 William Fullarton was granted a charter from Queen Anne to constitute a free port at Troon and form accommodation to receive vessels and charge a levy from all vessels landing or loading materials, it appears that little was done for nearly 100 years till the Duke of Portland started to develop the harbour, in 1808, and in 1815 a ship building yard was completed. In 1843 when the Duke leased it to the Troon Shipbuilding Company, who carried on building ships till 1885 when the Ailsa Building Company took over, which was subsequently nationalised, as most other yards were. With the run down of ship-building in Scotland it was sold to an Australian businessman who still runs it, but on a much smaller scale.

A well-known landmark 'The Ballast Bank' was started about 1865 to form a shelter against storms and high tides for the harbour area. As its name suggests it was built from ballast, a lot of which came from ships arriving in the harbour to pick up their cargoes of coal, timber etc., which they transported to Ireland, the Americas and other parts of the world. Troon was at one time one of the busiest ports on the west coast of Scotland.

Troon has over its years had an industrial life such as

shipbuilding, railway repair depot, ship breaking, saltworks and a sawmill, but sadly most of these have now gone.

The Duke of Portland's name still lives today in the name of streets such as Portland Street, Portland Terrace and Titchfield Road; also one of the oldest hotels, up till a few years ago was named the Portland Arms, the original hotel on that site was built by the Duke in 1812. It burnt down in 1847; later on it was rebuilt as we now know it.

In front of the Portland Arms was the passenger terminus for the first railway in Scotland, the Troon to Kilmarnock line, which was built by the Duke to transport coal from his mines near Kilmarnock to Troon harbour for export. The first waggons were pulled by horses, later on by one of the first steam engines, known as 'The Duke'. At a later time passengers were carried one shilling (five pence) being the fare for a return ticket Troon to Kilmarnock sitting inside.

Early in the 19th century Troon started to grow, many wealthy ship owners and merchants moved to Troon and built large houses. One was Charles Marr, who died in 1909 and left his estate for the benefit of the children of Troon, to further their education. Sir Alexander Walker, the managing director of Johnnie Walkers whisky firm in Kilmarnock, took over the management of the Trust, thereby ensuring that not only did Troon have a splendid College, but also a large fund for the future well-being of the College and the pupils, i.e. bursaries, sport equipment etc.

In 1810 the population of Troon was 200, today it is more than 14,000, so Troon expanded greatly. Now it is more of a dormitery town for other industrial and commercial towns surrounding it, as far afield as Glasgow.

The foregoing is a small potted history of Troon which we hope will give an insight to Troonites old and new. We also hope you will enjoy our collections of 'Old Troon' from 1880 to 1930 in postcards. Our sincere thanks to the following: Walter W. Clearie, M.A. for authentication, Mrs. Hogg, Miss Hogg Jr., Flora Wilson and June Paterson for assistance and the use of some postcards.

Stewart Wyllie & James Wilson

On Troon Shore

1. On the beach at Troon, early 1900's. A crowd of happy children wearing clothes of the period. The bearded man was the boat hirer, he is wearing a deep sea bonnet and would have been a retired seafarer. In the distance in the centre of the picture is the area where Troon swimming pool was built in 1930/31 and later demolished in the 1980's.

The Esplanade, Troon

2. Troon Promenade, early 1900's. An excellent view of Portland Terrace and Titchfield Road with the band stand in the middle (notice how flat the ground is — raised shortly after this to protect the town from south-westerly gales).

ESPLANADE TROON.

3. Troon Esplanade 1900. This photograph is taken from the area known as McCubbins Gangways but long before his time, there is no band stand on the shore front, the grass banking in Portland Terrace is missing, presumably this is taken before the Troon floods. The banking was installed shortly after to protect the town. Note St. Clair Terrace are still not built.

Bathing Station, Troon.

4. 'The bathing station' at Betsy's Kirn, opposite the top end of Welbeck Crescent. It was used till the swimming pool opened in 1931 near by.

The Beach, Troon.

5. South Beach around 1920. The bathing huts in the rear were pulled to the waters edge by horses, hence the large wheels.

Band Stand with Pipe Band, Troon.

6. The band stand about 1908, with band performing. It was built in 1906 and demolished in 1959 to make way for the paddling pool.

Esplanade from South, Troon

Valentines Series

7. The Esplanade from the south with Troon in the background. As you can see there are no sand dunes, the crowd of people are buying ice cream from 'Tog's' Barrow in 1902 (Togneri is still in business). On the right is now a car park.

8. Craiglea Hotel, South Beach, taken from the shore side around 1926.

The Parish Church from the Esplanade,

Troon.

E 26244

9. The Parish Church from the Esplanade. An excellent view of the Esplanade taken around 1900. In the centre of the photograph is Villa Marine, demolished in the early 1970's to make way for luxury flats.

10. St. Meddans Street, 1909. St. Meddans Street, looking towards the sea. Little change in over eighty years, except that the gas lamps and iron railings have disappeared and milk is no longer delivered in barrels on a cart.

CHURCH STREET, TROON.

11. Bentinck Drive and Church Street around 1906. On the left is Mar Lodge Hotel. The name was taken to a new hotel in South Beach later on. As you see the St. Meddans Church has no clock, when it was built in 1888 till about 1926, when the church in the background was demolished and the clock removed to St. Meddans Church.

12. Dundonald Road looking west around 1929. On the right is Carrols Eplorium and Gordons grocers shop.

Bentinck Drive, Troon

13. Bentinck Drive looking north around 1906. It appears that a lot of building is going on as the road is still hard packed earth. The numbers 52, 67, 69 and Welbeck Hotel (now flats) are not yet built. The house on the right with the cross is 'Burnockside'.

Bentinck Drive, Troon

14. Milk ladies selling fresh milk from churns off her cart outside number 3 Bentinck Drive, around 1900.

Bentinck Drive, Troon

15. Bentinck Drive in 1909, when it was tree lined and houses had iron railings. The railings went towards the war effort 1939-1945 and the trees dissappeared in the 1950's, no doubt due to the increase of traffic.

PORTLAND STREET, TROON.

16. Portland Street looking towards the sea in 1923. On the left was Whites Newsagent (now Menzies). Beyond is the 'Picture House' (now Woolworths). It was the first of Troons three picture houses to close in the early 1950's.

WEST PORTLAND STREET, TROON

17. West Portland Street from the shore end around 1930. At the centre left is the Beach Café, beyond is 'Kirkwoods' bakery, later a supermarket, now three shop units.

The Cross and Ayr St., Troon

18. Troon Cross around 1924. Young lads with a horse and cart turn into Ayr Street. Note the policeman standing in the middle of the road.

19. Troon Cross looking from Templehill around 1900. On the left is the two storey building with the pub, not long before its demolition. Beyond are new shops and houses above
in Ayr Street. The road is still not yet tarred.

20. Troon Cross early 1880. To the right is Templehill, left is West Postland Street. The shop on the corner is Whites bakery shop.

"The Troon Flood," 26th Nov., 1912.

PHOTO BY A. SHERRIFFS, M.P.S.
CHEMIST, TROON.

21. Troon flood, 26th November 1912. A day to remember for the residents of Troon when due to south-westerly gales and high tides the town was flooded at a height of 2 ft at the cross. The photograph was taken by Sheriffs the chemist, whose premises were at 19/21 Ayr Street, Troon.

THE CROSS, TROON. (ABOUT THE YEAR 1889.)

22. Troon Cross 1880's. An early view of Troon Cross in 1880. The two storey building on the left hand side at the time of the photograph was a public house (Cunningham's pub). This building was knocked down around the turn of the century and replaced by the current four storey building 1902-03. To the right of this is a garden wall which was knocked down and was replaced by the current shops with flats above, commencing at number 17 Ayr Street in 1900. The back wall and roof of the Old Academy can be seen beyond the garden wall in the centre of the postcard.

Portland Street, Troon

23. Portland Street, Troon. View of Troon taken around 1900. This photograph also shows the railway bridge near Dodds garage and also the spire of the United Free Church which was at that time situated on the corner of Portland Street and Church Street, but was knocked down some years later and replaced with current shops and the present post office.

Ayr Street, Troon.

24. Ayr Street, Troon. Looking down Ayr Street from South Beach little has changed from 1900, with exception that the house on the left hand side of the photograph was demolished and replaced by Troon Town Hall in 1932. Troon post office was sited in Ayr Street in 1900 to 1901, being moved in 1911 to Portland Street and then in 1930 to its current site in Church Street.

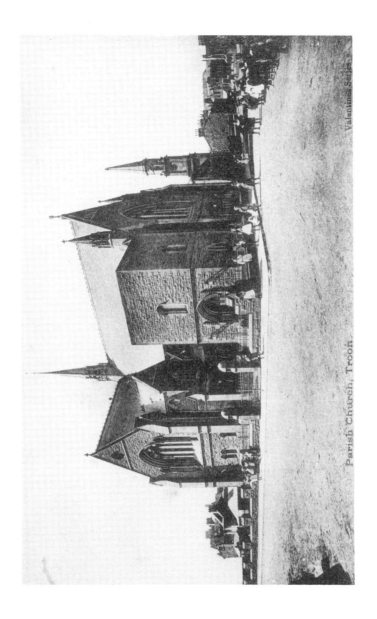

Parish Church, Troon

Valentines Series

25. Troon Parish Church (1900). An excellent photograph of Troon Parish Church built in 1895. The steeple at the rear of the church has since been removed as it fell into disrepair, presumably due to the high winds and salt water damage over the years. On the left hand of the church is Marine Cottage, which was knocked down in the early 1970's to make way for new luxury flats known as Marine View Court.

Unionist Club Buildings and Templehill, Troon.

RELIABLE SERIES. R1793

26. Unionist Club buildings and Templehill, Troon, taken from West Portland Street corner in 1910. The lamp standard with the drinking well was a gas lamp and it remained at the Cross until the late 1940's before being replaced by an electric street lamp.

27. The Esplanade Troon, 1908. An excellent photograph showing the Troon bandstand which was built on the Esplanade in the early 1900's. The gentleman with the bicycle in the foreground would be unable to stand at this point now as this area of ground was lifted to protect the town from south westerly gales which flooded Troon.

Caulking the "Wildwood" in Troon Dry Dock

28. The 'Wildwood' in dock at Troon for caulking and repairs in the 1890's. The 'Wildwood' was built in Canada in 1883 — gross tonnage 1573 — length 222.3, port of registration St. John, New Brunswick. She plied between Canada and Scotland on a regular basis with timber etc.

Templehill, Troon

4319. 6.

29. Templehill, Troon. Templehill was the site of the Duke of Portlands Hotel, built in 1812 – known as the Portland Arms Hotel. This was also a coaching house and as it was near the harbour presumably would be used by ship owners and sea farers. Opposite the hotel was the terminal for the Troon to Kilmarnock Railway, built in 1825, first as a horse-drawn tramway and later tramcars were drawn by Stevenson's steam driven locomotive known locally as the Duke. On the right hand side of the photograph is the 'bank building' which originally housed the Union Bank of Scotland before it moved to the Unionist building at Troon Cross which is now the Bank of Scotland.

30. Lady Isle Lighthouse off Troon about 1908. A small house has since been built. A few ships have been wrecked in storms on the isle. For some years now Lady Isle has been a bird sanctuary, and is also home for a small colony of grey seals.

The Welfare Home, Templehill, Troon.

31. Miners Welfare Home at the top of Templehill around 1930. This house was once owned by Adam Wood, a shipyard manager, and was known as Portland Villa.

32. Junction of Harbour Road and Templehill about 1905. A walled garden was later formed on the right. The road appears to be untarred, on the right is the co-operative shop, to the left The Knowe Hotel and Harbour Bar.

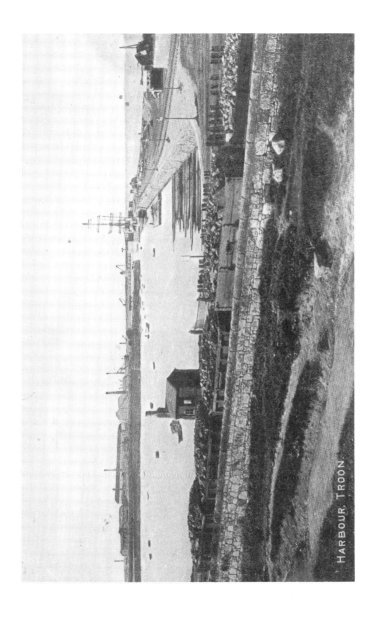

HARBOUR. TROON.

33. Troon Harbour, 1900. Troon Harbour from the top of Templehill looking over the inner basin to Troon Shipyard. The inner basin at that time was used as a logging area with a saw mill near where the current Marina Office is situated. On the right hand side are the railway line and coal landing quay, the railway line being the first in Scotland.

The Gardens, Troon

34. The top of Templehill around 1925, the houses were built about 1845. In the centre is the Co-op shop, to the left is the Knowe and Harbour Bar. The walled park was known as 'Morneys Park'. This was donated by Adam Wood of Portland Villa.

The "Scotia" in Troon Harbour

35. The 'Scotia' in Troon Harbour around 1915. The 'Scotia' was powered by sail and steam, this was the ship that took Scott to the Antartic.

36. Paddle steamer 'Juno' and tug boat the 'Troon' with many sail powered ships, in the outer harbour around 1910.

37. Postcard of the Exchange Building with a small grocers shop to the left hand side. Both these buildings were demolished in the 1930's, when the ground was taken over by Allan Wood, ship owner, who owned the adjacent building which we now know as the Miners Welfare Home. The Exchange House was called thus as it was the information and shipping office for the port of Troon.

The Ladies' Golf House, Troon

38. The Ladies Golf Club House, Crosbie Road, about 1900. At the top left is Piersland Lodge, to the right Landale, before the trees were planted. The white hut is Portland Golf Club House.

Troon from Golf Course

39. Troon from the Marine Hotel in 1902. In the foreground the now Royal Troon Golf Club House, behind it flats are now built (Crosbie Court). Beyond that is Crosbie Towers.

Troon. The Golf Club House and Marine Hotel.

E 26247

40. Royal Troon Golf Club House around 1902. The starters box is in front of the building. On the right is the Marine Hotel which was built in the 1890's.

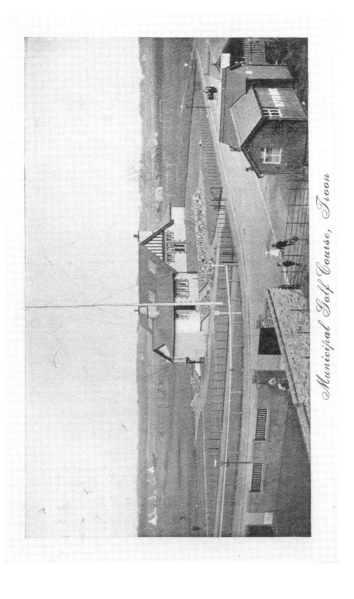

Municipal Golf Course, Troon

41. A slightly larger Municipal Club House photographed in 1922. In the foreground is Willie Fernie, club makers shop. To the left in the background is 'the Bogs Cottages', to the right the football park and beyond it the polo park. As you see there is no Willockston Road or Golf Crescent Houses.

Troon Municipal Golf Course—The Warren

42. Troon Municipal Golf Course around the turn of the century. The postcard mentions that this area is the 'warren'. This hole is positioned where Colonel W. Fullarton's established a large man-made warren for rabbits to ensure that Fullarton House had fresh meat throughout the year, as there were no fridges in those days. In addition the gamekeeper sold the skins for additional income. The Warren is the area behind Fullarton Drive and the dovecote was situated between the 12th and 13th hole.

Troon Municipal Golf Club House

T. M. & W. IRVINE, Photographers, Troon

43. Taken in 1910, a very small Municipal Golf Club House. To the left is the Tudor style Railway Station.

44. Troon Municipal Golf Club House 1912-1913. A view taken from Golf Crescent from the railway embankment. The roadway would appear to have been hard packed earth track. On the Harling Drive corner there is a flagpole which has disappeared over the years.

Municipal Golf Club House and Crescent, Troon.

45. The Municipal Golf Club House 1926-1928. Troon Municipal Golf Club House and Golf Crescent with excellent detail of the golf professionals sheds. In front of the club house there are four artillery guns presumably left over from the First World War.

Cottage in South Wood, Troon.

46. This must have been one of the most beautiful thatched houses built in Troon. It is at the entrance to Frognal House in the south woods and was built in 1910.

MARINE HOTEL TROON.

47. Marine Hotel 1895. An early photo of the Marine Hotel which has been altered on numerous occasions over the years to its now present state. The building to the left hand side was originally the staff quarters and the Marine & Bogend Garage which has now been converted into a restaurant with adjoining health centre.

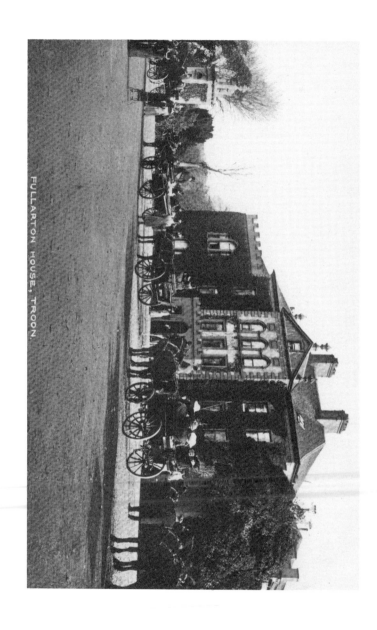

FULLARTON HOUSE, TROON.

48. A social event at Fullarton House in 1914. The house was built in 1745 and sadly demolished due to rot in 1966. The pillars on the left and right still remain, the court yard, stables and stores are now dwelling houses.

49. The 'dove cot' to the east of the 12th tee on Lochgreen Golf Course around the turn of the century. Due to its dangerous condition it was demolished around 1960.

50. Fullarton Court Yard around 1922. On the left is a Rol s Royce with its driver Mr. Brown, to the right is a Napier, the driver was Mr. Gibson.

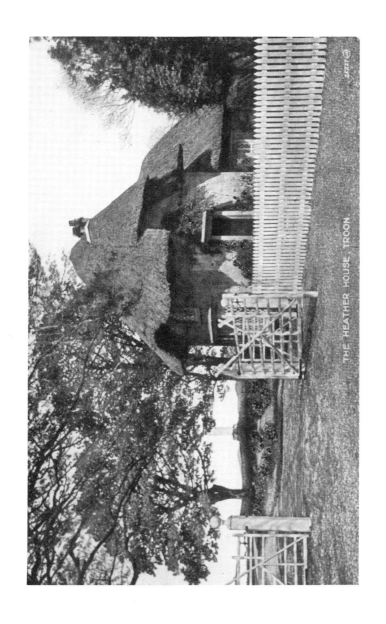

THE HEATHER HOUSE, TROON

51. Pictured in 1897 the 'Heather House' at the entrance to Fullarton House on Isle of Pins Road. It was destroyed by fire in March 1958. The pillar seen through the gates was where the Fullartons dispensed their justice.

Old Row, Fullarton, Troon.

52. Old Row, Fullarton, Troon (1910), previously known as 'Old Causeyside', built for workers of the Fullarton estates, now known as the Isle of Pins Road.

BARASSIE. TROON

53. Barassie around 1910. The houses in Barassie were originally built by Kilmarnock business men as summer homes for themselves and their families and at one time they had a private bowling green, but eventually their interest turned to golf. They then built Kilmarnock and Barassie Golf Club, north of the Barassie railway junction. The house on the right hand side of the photograph was known as the Towers and is now the Towers Hotel.

Troon, Templehill.

E. 26248

54. Templehill from The Cross, 1905. Templehill was not only the centre of commerce and business, it was a busy shopping area and this photograph shows the Bank of Scotland building with the Unionist Halls above built in 1894-95.

The Cross, Troon

55. The Cross, Troon 1906. The Cross is the commercial part of the town and at the time the main thoroughfare being Templehill leading to the Harbour, which was a busy coal exporting port in the early 1800's. This is an extremely interesting postcard as you will see the Ailsa Bar is a single storey building situated where Togs Café is now. The Ailsa Bar then moved to the building on the right and is still in existence as a public house to this day.

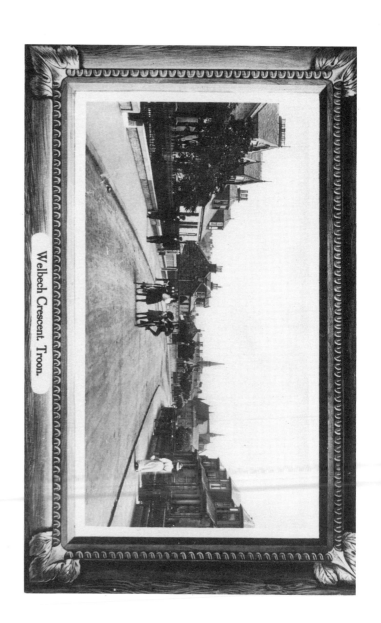

Welbech Crescent, Troon.

56. Welbeck Crescent, Troon, 1910. Little has changed over eighty years – children still playing in the street with their bicycles. It is an interesting point that some of the houses on the right hand side of this photograph have two front doors. This was to allow the family to split the house into an upstairs and downstairs situation for letting to summer visitors in the hey days when Troon was one of the most popular resorts in the Clyde.

St. Medden's Street,

Troon.

E 26246

57. St. Meddans Street in 1900. Not a lot has changed, except the railings from the front of the houses have now gone, the lamp standards are now electric, the church now has a clock.

Troon, Ayr Street.

E 26243

58. Ayr Street, Troon, 1903. A summers afternoon in Ayr Street with pedestrians, horses and carts and a young boy on a bicycle. Notice the sun blinds out all the way along the street and the salt fish barrel on the pavement outside the fish shop

SOUTH BEACH LOOKING SOUTH, TROON.

RELIABLE SERIES 1076

59. A horse and cart passing the South Beach Hotel around about 1905.

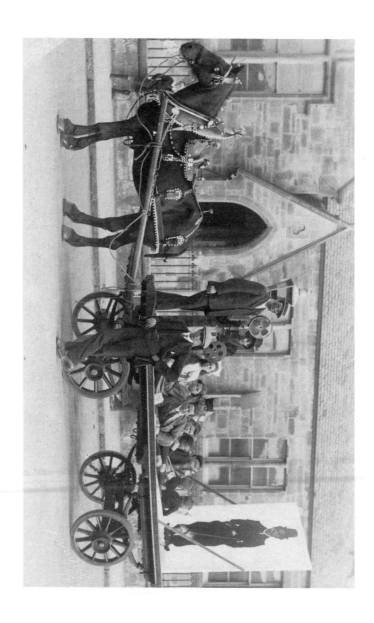

60. Red Cross Week 1918. Outside Troon Primary (the Wee School) with local children all enjoying themselves in the back of a local carriers wagon. The old original Troon Academy being sited approximately 500 yards behind the health centre shop in Academy Street. This was not the first school in Troon, it being in Dundonald Road now the Marr College Gardiners House at no 97. Dundonald Road opened in the 1800's for the children of Troon.

THE STATION TROON.

61. Troon Railway Station. Troon Railway Station is an interesting building being built in 1892 in a Tudor design. This is in fact the second Troon station, the first being built in 1839 at Dundonald Road near Marr College. The station was modernised in 1985-1987 and the railway bridge shown here was removed to increase the height for the new electric locomotives.

MARR COLLEGE, TROON.

964

62. Marr College 1935. An early photo view of Marr College taken shortly after it opened, the College being built on the farm known as Wallacefield Farm. The College was gifted to the children of Troon by the late Charles Kerr Marr (born October 1855 — died 1919). The motto of the College is 'Hic Patet In Geniis Campus' (this field lies open to talent). In addition large playing fields lie to the east of the College.

Fullarton House, Troon.

63. Fullarton House built in 1745. A superb view of a beautiful house which was knocked down in the 1950's as it had fallen into disrepair and at that time no-one felt it was worth saving. The courtyard to the rear is still standing and has been converted into luxury mews type homes. The gate towers still remain and the garden area to the rear remains as a well kept park for Troon residents.

ENTRANCE TO SOUTH WOOD, TROON.

64. Entrance to South Wood, Troon. A view of South Woods Road and gatehouse of Auchenkyle around 1910.

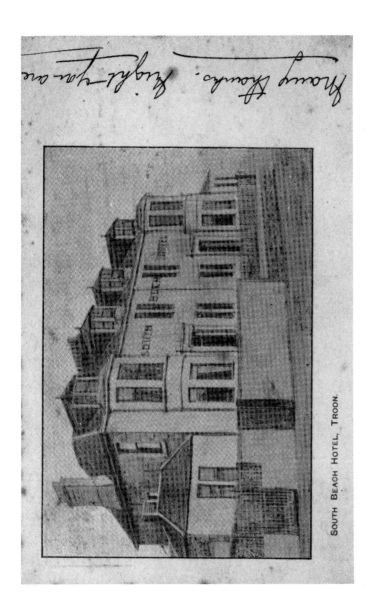

SOUTH BEACH HOTEL, TROON.

65. South Beach Hotel, South Beach, Troon, around 1900. This photograph clearly shows that the property could possibly have been two large semi-detached houses at one time before being altered to a hotel. This property has been modified numerous times over the years with addition of a public bar to the far right. Dining and function rooms were also added over a period of years.

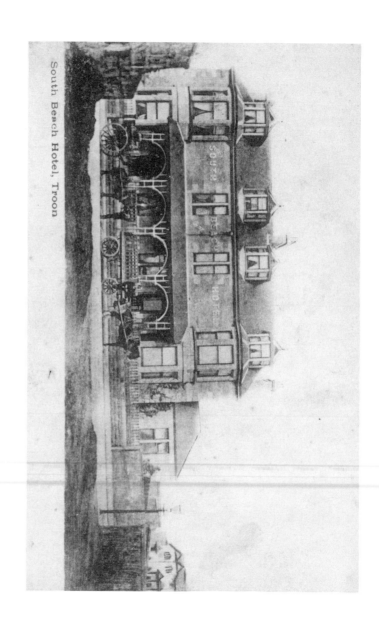

South Beach Hotel, Troon

66. South Beach Hotel, Troon, early 1900's. This is an interesting postcard, a small veranda having been built on the front of the hotel. Also in the postcard horse-drawn carts owned by the GSWR Railway Company. The hotel being only five minutes from the railway station and two minutes from the beach made it very popular with holidaymakers.

Mar Lodge, St. Meddaus Street, Troon

67. Marr Lodge Hotel, St. Meddans Street, Troon. The hotel was situated at the corner of St. Meddans Street and Bentinck Drive. The property was later divided into two houses and at a later date another Marr Lodge guest house was built in South Beach. It also was later closed as a guest house in 1970 and turned into flats.

St. Meddans Street, Troon.

68. St. Meddans Street. St. Meddans Street was built mainly in the late 1890's with some houses near the beach end being built much earlier. This view is looking due west towards the sea and on the top left hand corner of the postcard is clearly shown the Troon Burgh coat of arms. Troon became a burgh in 1897 and the arms show clearly Troon's link with sea, railway and industry.

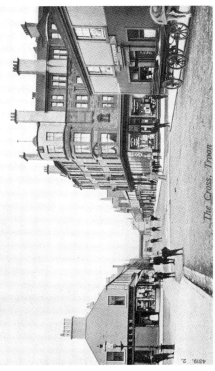

69. Above: The Cross from West Portland Street (1909). The photographer has managed to have some of the locals pose for him in the middle of the picture the railway bridge over Portland Street leading from Troon Railway Station to the harbour can be clearly seen. This bridge was removed in 1973 when the line fell into disuse.

Beneath: St. Meddans Church, built in 1888. This photograph taken in 1900 shows the congregation at that time had still not subscribed sufficient funds to install the clock on the spire. The postcard also shows in the bottom right hand corner of the picture the spire of the U.F. Church built in 1856, the present site of John Menzies and the post office. The building on the left hand of the picture was the Marr Lodge Hotel.

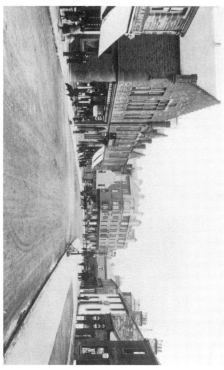

Cross Roads, Loans

70. Above: Troon 1910, a photograph of Templehill looking towards the Cross and Ayr Street. There is little change in the shopping area to this date with the exception that the single storey building on the right hand side was replaced in the early 1930's by a picture house and in the late 1950's by a bowling alley and in the mid-1980's a chemist shop.

Beneath: Cross Road Loans around 1930. The house on the left was known as the toll house, probably it was the site of the old toll at Loans. Behind the houses on the right can be seen 'Bennies' Greenhouses.

The Pierrots at Ballast Bank, Troon

71. 'Dad Lindsays Pierrots' performing at the south end of Ballast Bank in 1907 before the harbour scheme was built. Top left is the back of Welbeck Crescent and to the left is Portland Villa, now Miners Welfare Home.

The Loans, Troon

72. Loans Village, Troon, around 1904. The blacksmith on the left is a Mr. Fullarton. The Fullartons were in business for many generations as blacksmiths in Loans. The shop is now a garage.

Barassie.

73. New Bank Barassie around 1900, later named Beach Road. The above houses on the north side of Burn were built around 1866. As you see there is no road to the front of the houses. To the right is the old bank with 'the towers' at the far end.

BURNFOOT, BARASSIE, TROON.

Volunteer Camp, Lochgreen, Troon. ("The Dinner Hour.")

74. Above: Burnfoot Farm and camp site at Barassie around 1930. On the shore side of the farm is Burnfoot Tea Room. Burnfoot Farm was demolished in the 1950s to make way for a council estate which now covers the whole area shown.

Beneath: Little is known about this card posted in 1906. The caption says Volunteer Camp, Lochgreen (the dinner hour). There are men in uniform, one lady and children?

Troon Burgh Military Band.

75. 'Troon Burgh Military Band' in the first quarter of this century.

The Gyaws, Troon.

76. The Gyaws, Troon, 1900's. The Gyaws were situated on the old Troon Golf Course at the green keepers house on the site next to the Suncourt Hotel. This is an early postcard and it was a tradition in the early days for people to write on the front of the card.